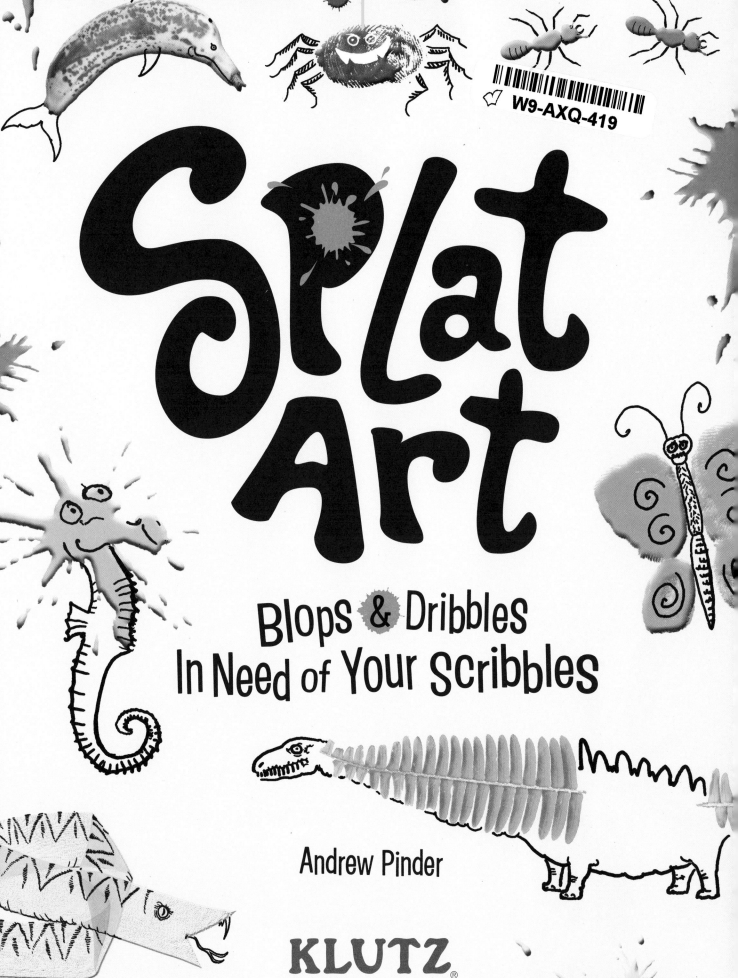

Splat Art

Blops & Dribbles In Need of Your Scribbles

Andrew Pinder

KLUTZ

KLUTZ

KLUTZ creates activity books and other great stuff for kids ages 3 to 103. We began our corporate life in 1977 in a garage we shared with a Chevrolet Impala. Although we've outgrown that first office, Klutz galactic headquarters remains in Palo Alto, California, and we're still staffed entirely by real human beings. For those of you who collect mission statements, here's ours:
Create wonderful things • Be good • Have fun

WRITE US

We would love to hear your comments regarding this or any of our books. We have many!

KLUTZ, 450 Lambert Avenue, Palo Alto, CA 94306

Printed in Korea. 91

Created by Andrew Pinder
First published in Great Britain in 2011 by Buster Books,
an imprint of Michael O'Mara Books Limited, 9 Lion Yard,
Tremadoc Road, London SW4 7NQ
www.mombooks.com/busterbooks
Copyright © 2011 Buster Books.

Distributed in the UK by
Scholastic UK Ltd
Westfield Road
Southam, Warwickshire
England CV47 0RA

Distributed in Australia by
Scholastic Australia Ltd
PO Box 579
Gosford, NSW
Australia 2250

Distributed in Canada by
Scholastic Canada Ltd
604 King Street West
Toronto, Ontario
Canada M5V 1E1

ISBN 978-0-545-42482-0
UPC 7-30767-42482-4

4 1 5 8 5 7 0 8 8 8

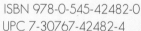

VISIT OUR WEBSITE

You can check out all the stuff we make, find a nearby retailer, request a catalog, sign up for a newsletter, e-mail us, or just goof off!
www.klutz.com

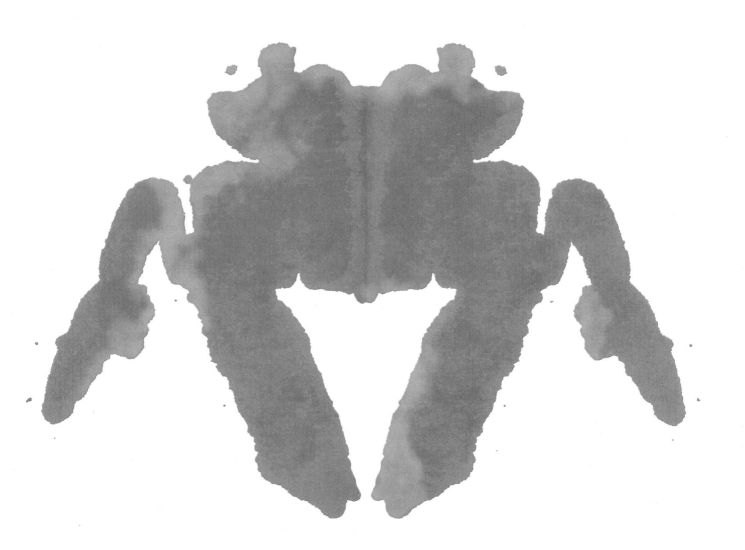

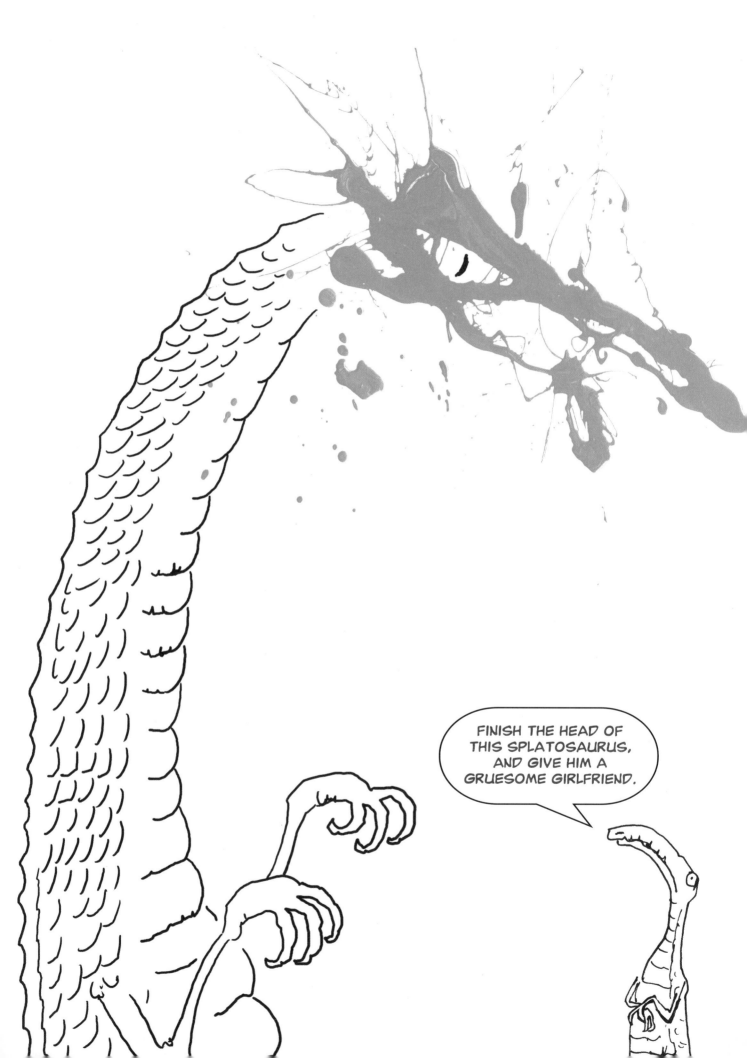

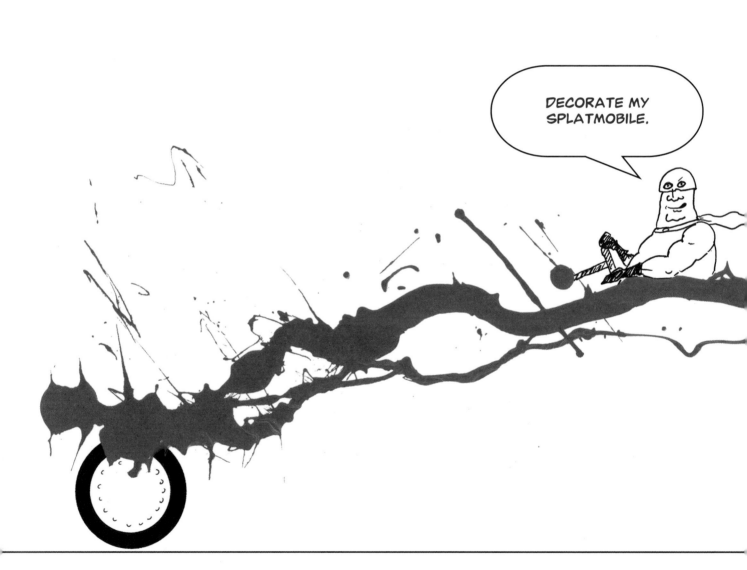

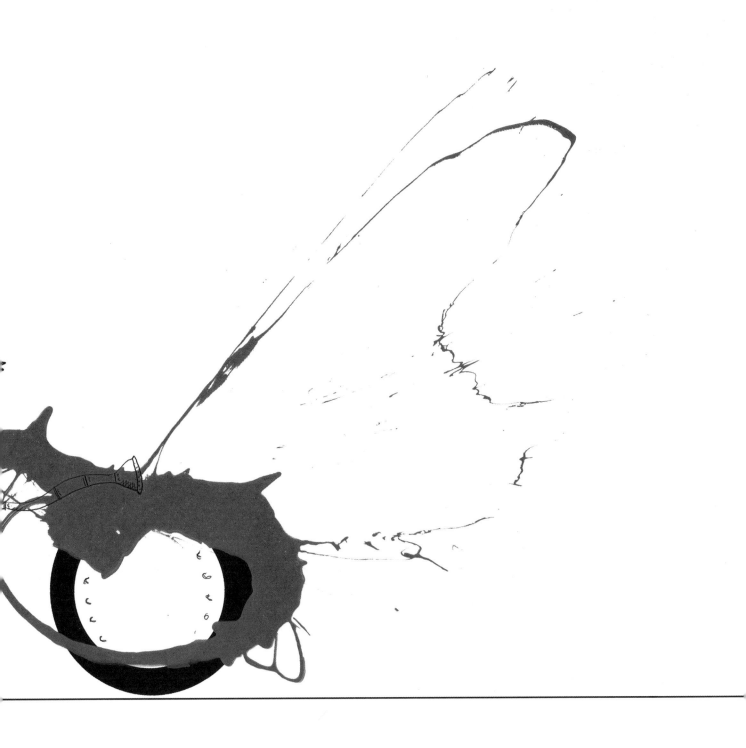

TURN THE FRILLY FERNS INTO DINOSAUR BONES.

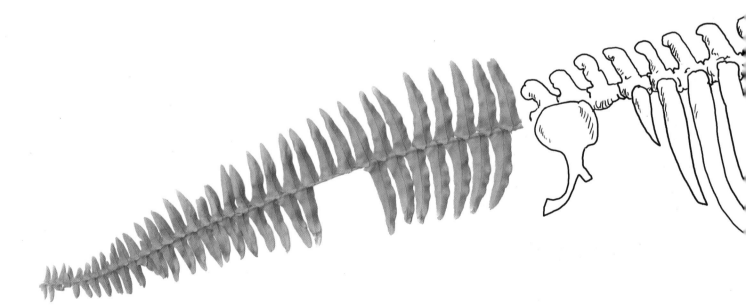

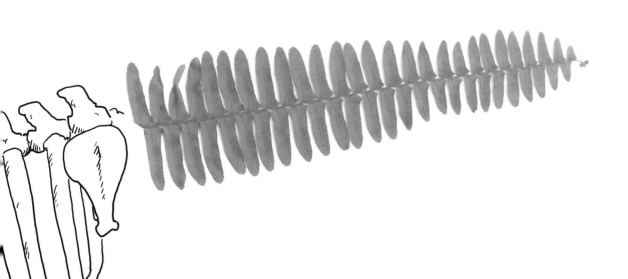

GIVE US SILLY FACES AND EVEN SILLIER NAMES.

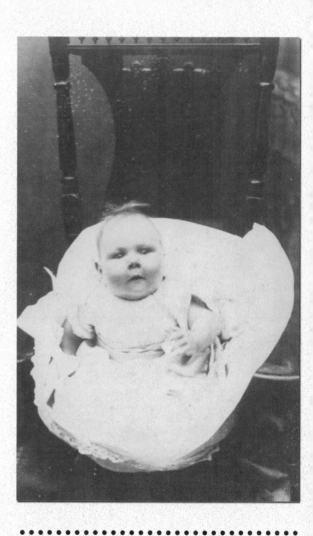

DRAW FAIRIES UNDER THE PRETTY PETAL HATS.

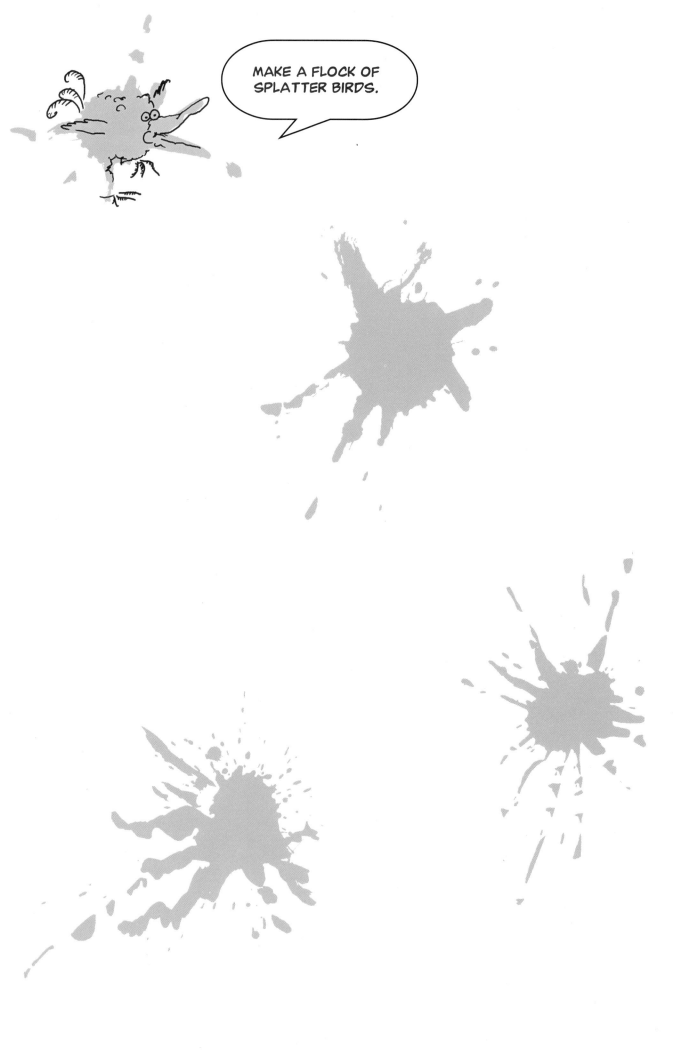

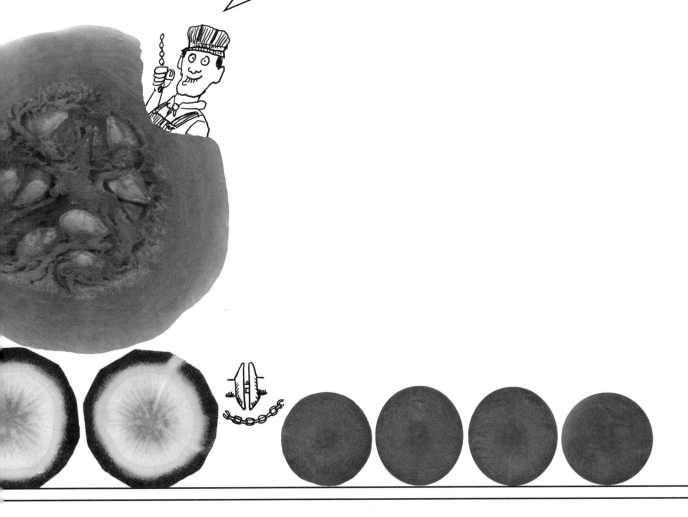

DRAW BODIES FOR THESE THUMBPRINT BUTTERFLIES.

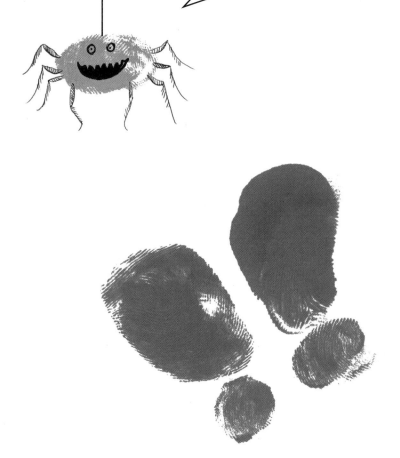

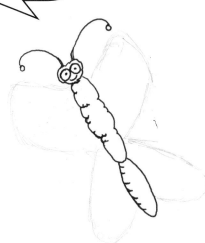

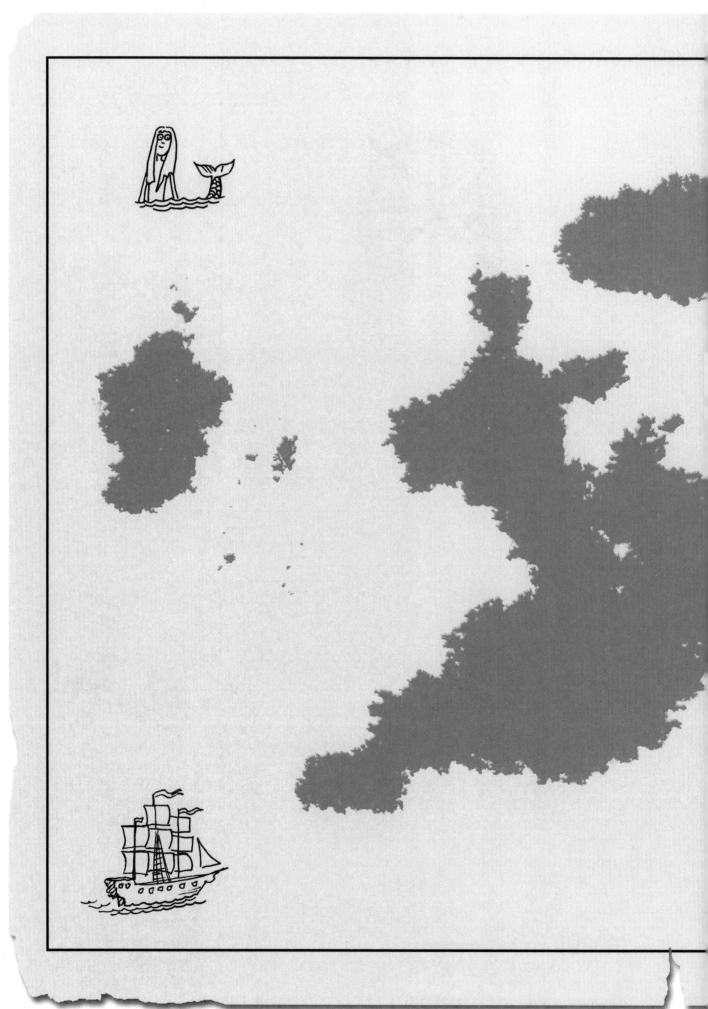

TURN THE DRIPS INTO HAIRY BEASTS, LIKE ME.

I AM A BRAINY ALIEN FROM THE PLANET CABBAGE. DRAW ME A FRIEND.

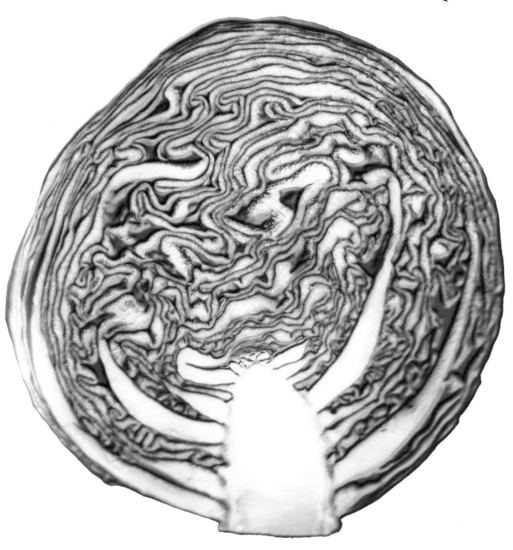

WELCOME TO PAPEROPOLIS. (I HOPE YOU DO WINDOWS.)

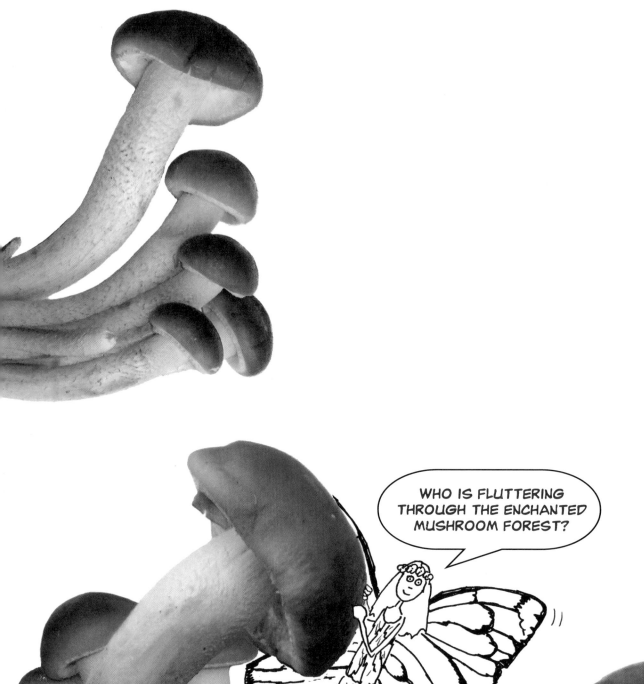

TURN THE
SPLATS INTO CUTE
ANIMALS, LIKE ME.

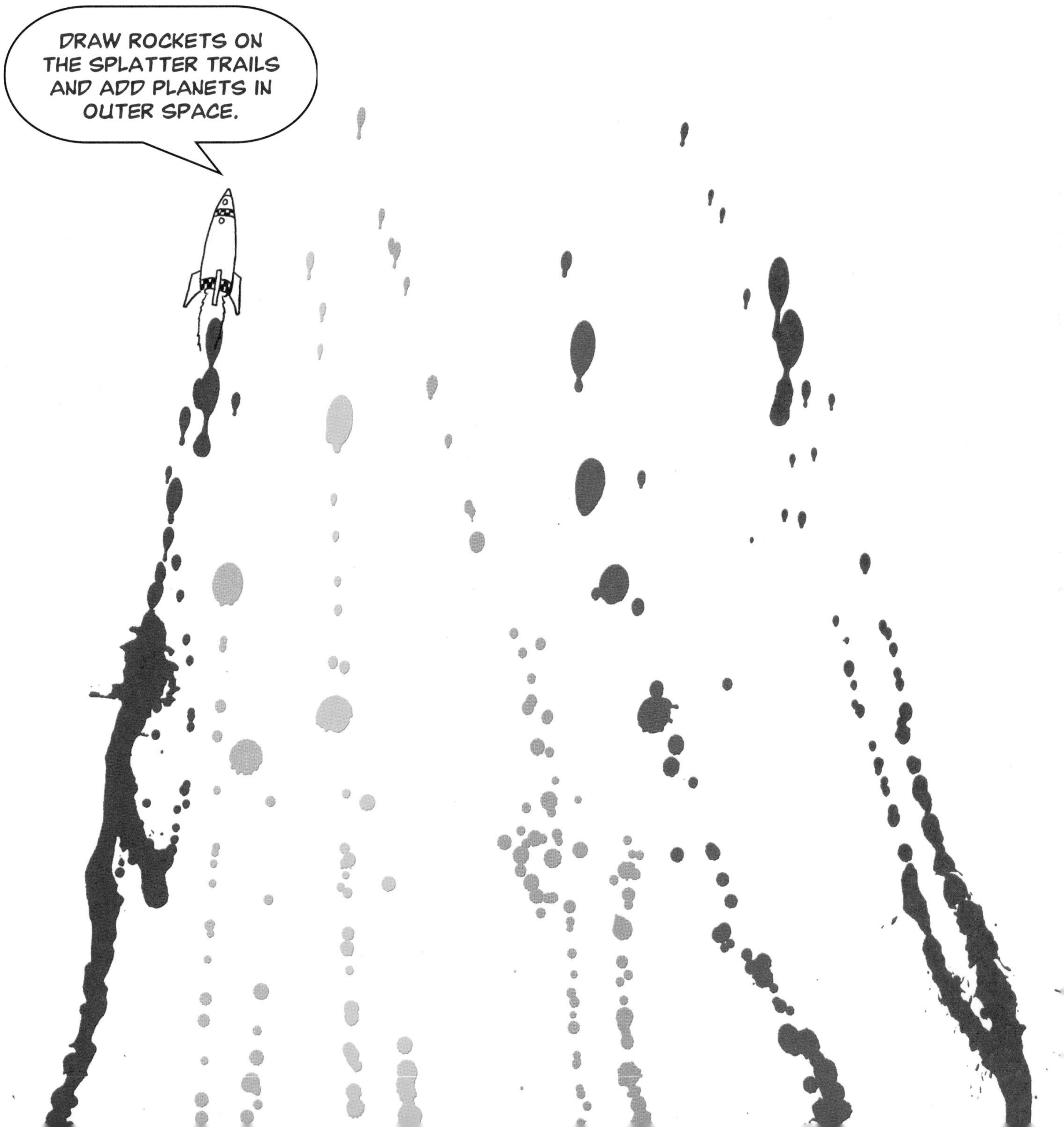
DRAW ROCKETS ON THE SPLATTER TRAILS AND ADD PLANETS IN OUTER SPACE.

MAKE THE LEAVES
INTO BEAUTIFUL
BIRDS, LIKE ME.

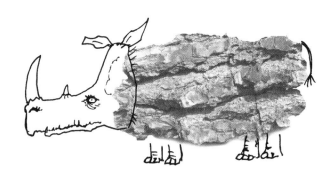

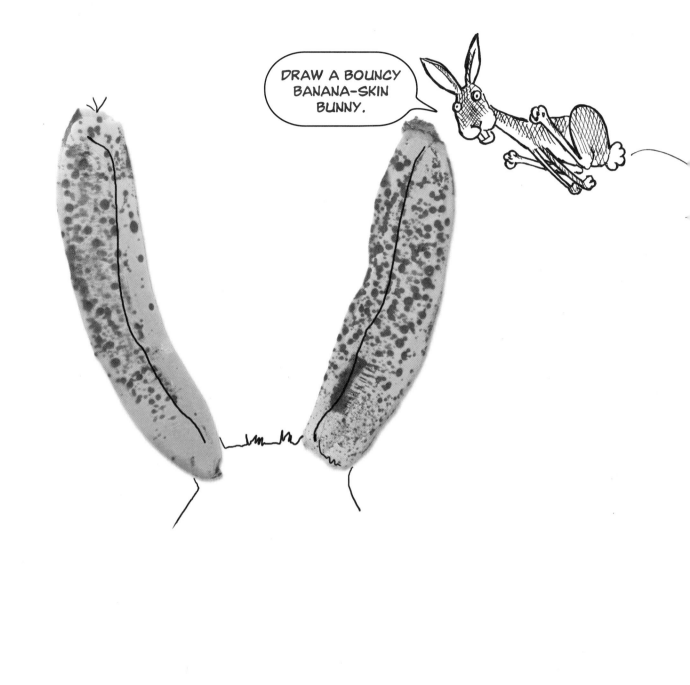

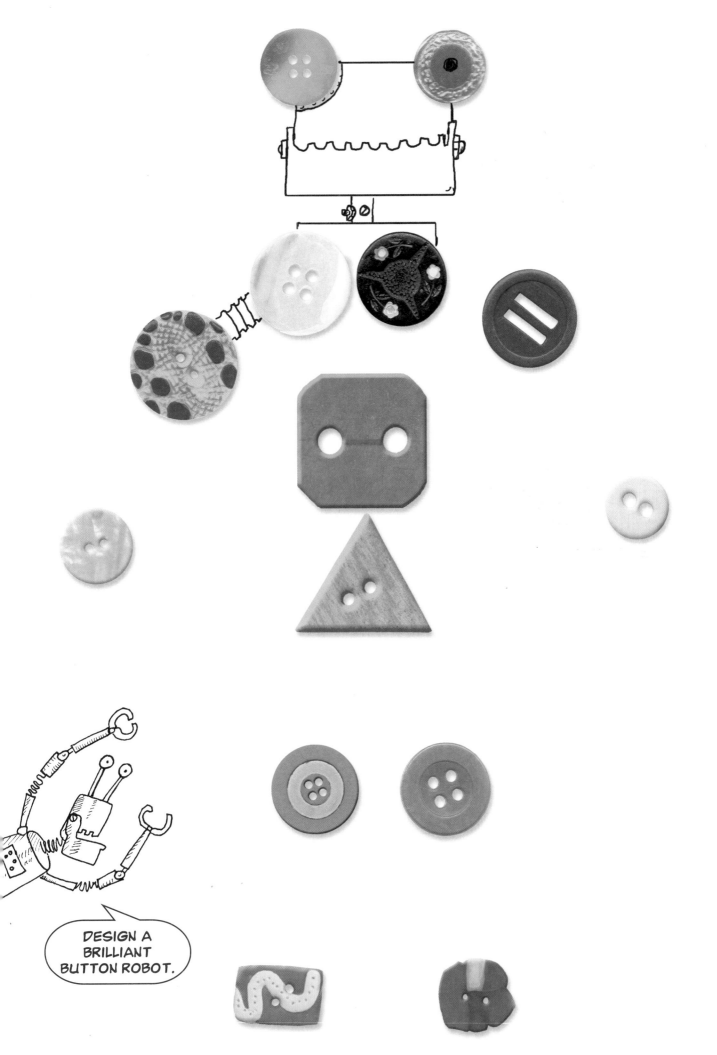

DESIGN A BRILLIANT BUTTON ROBOT.

FINISH DRAWING MY
FEATHERED FRIEND.

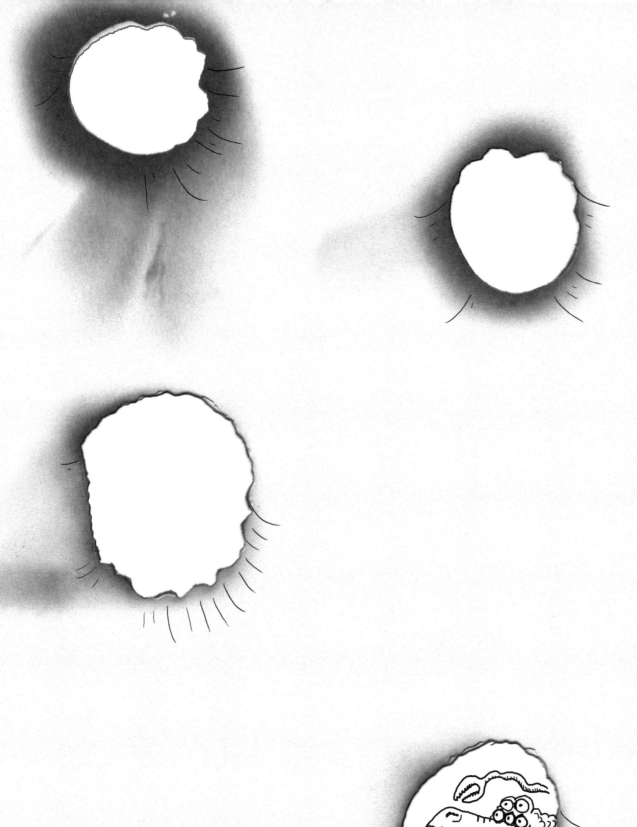
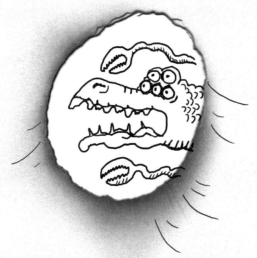

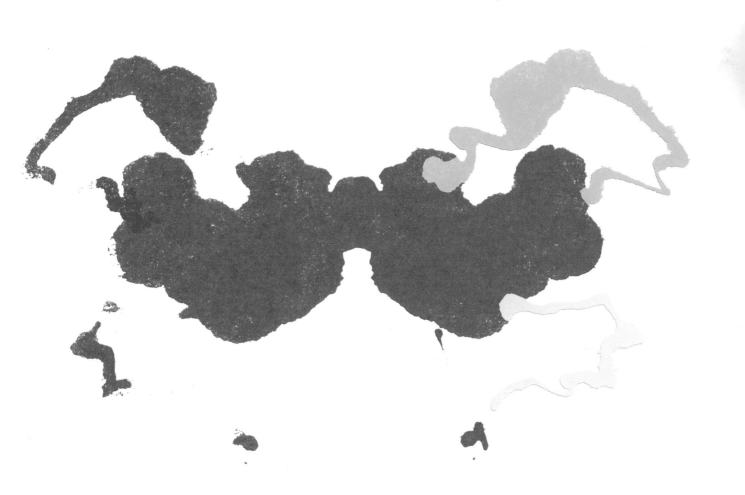

STORM COMING!
DRAW MORE PEOPLE
BRAVING THE WET,
WILD WIND.

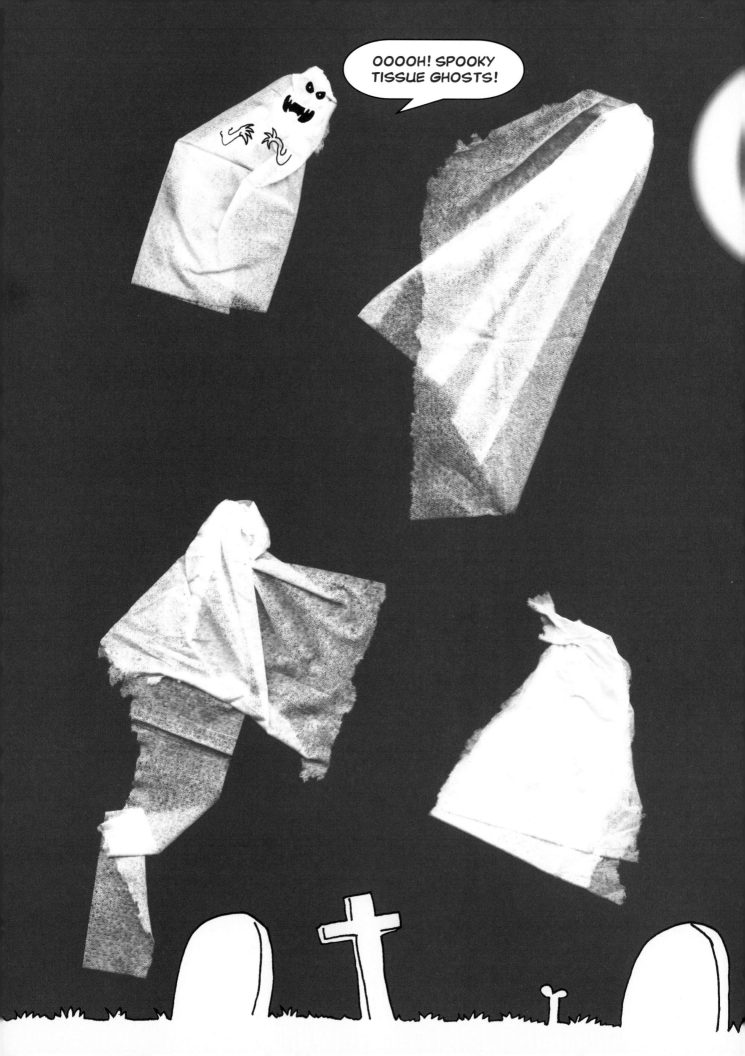

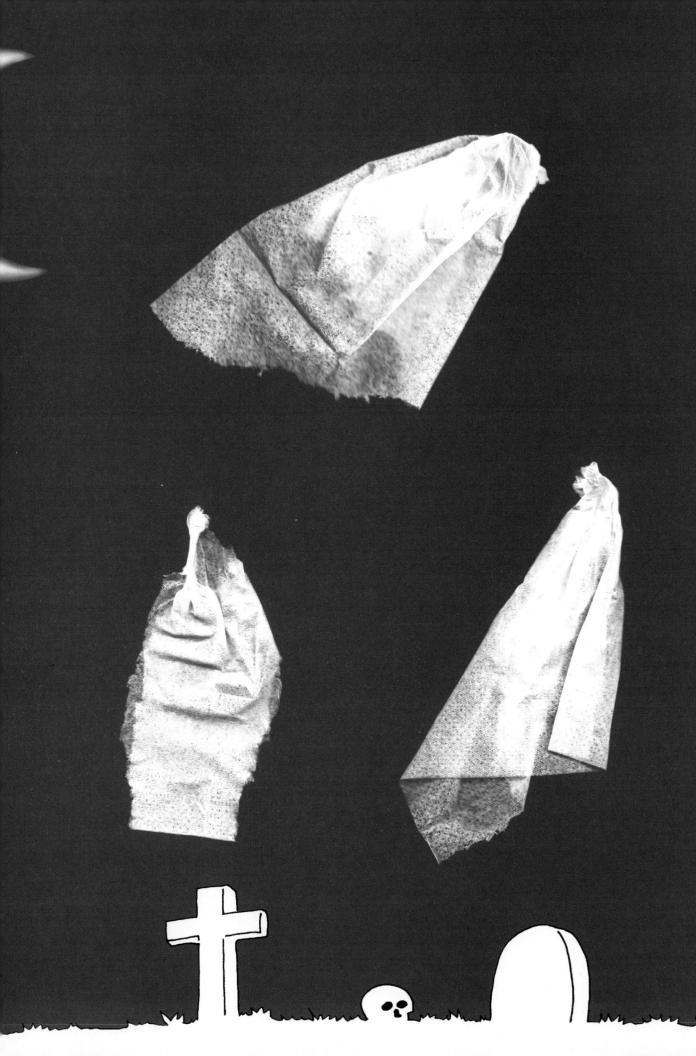

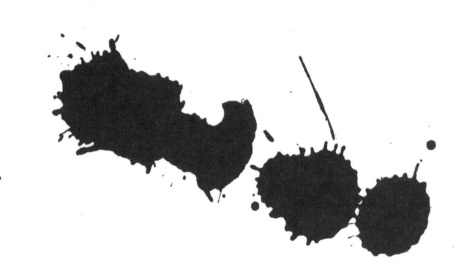

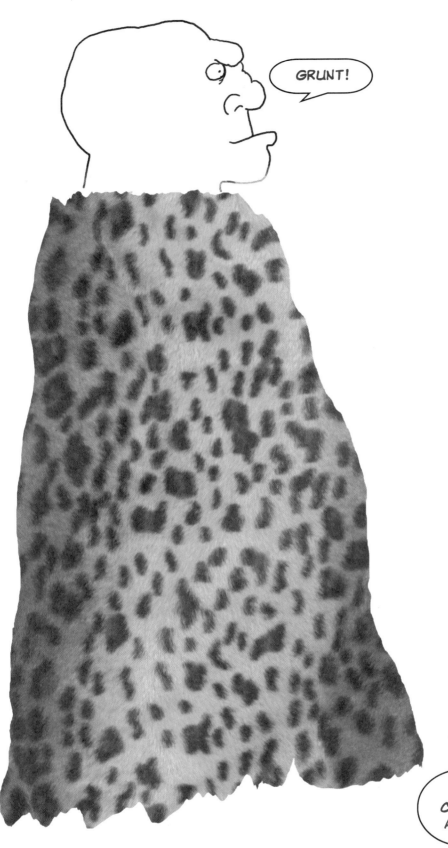

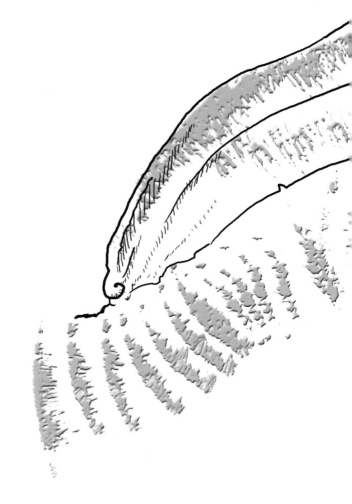

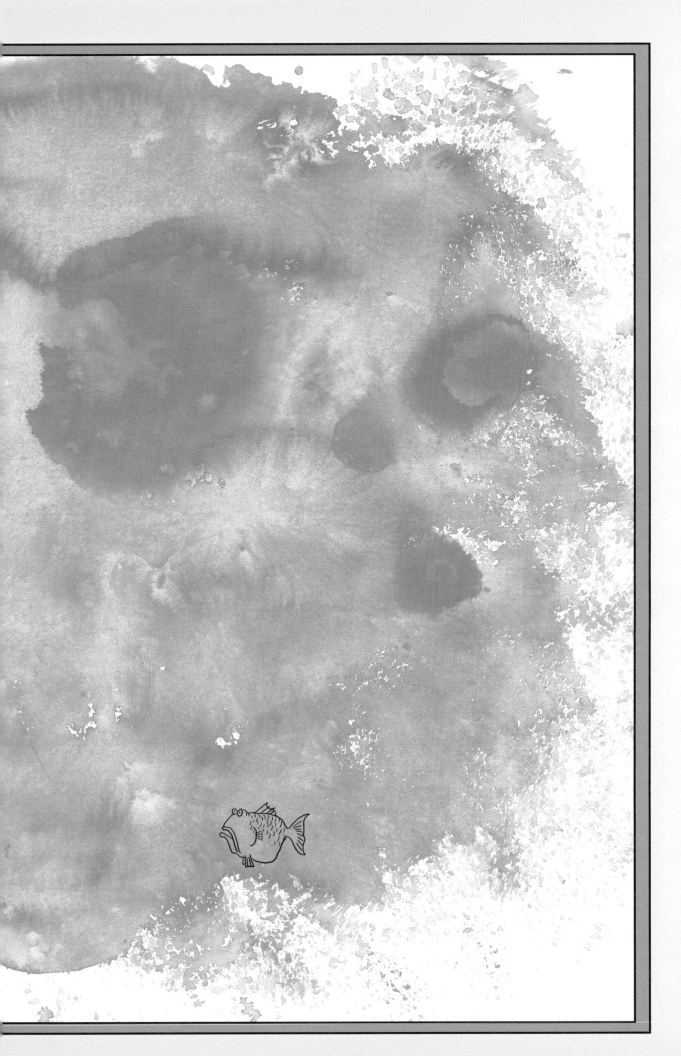

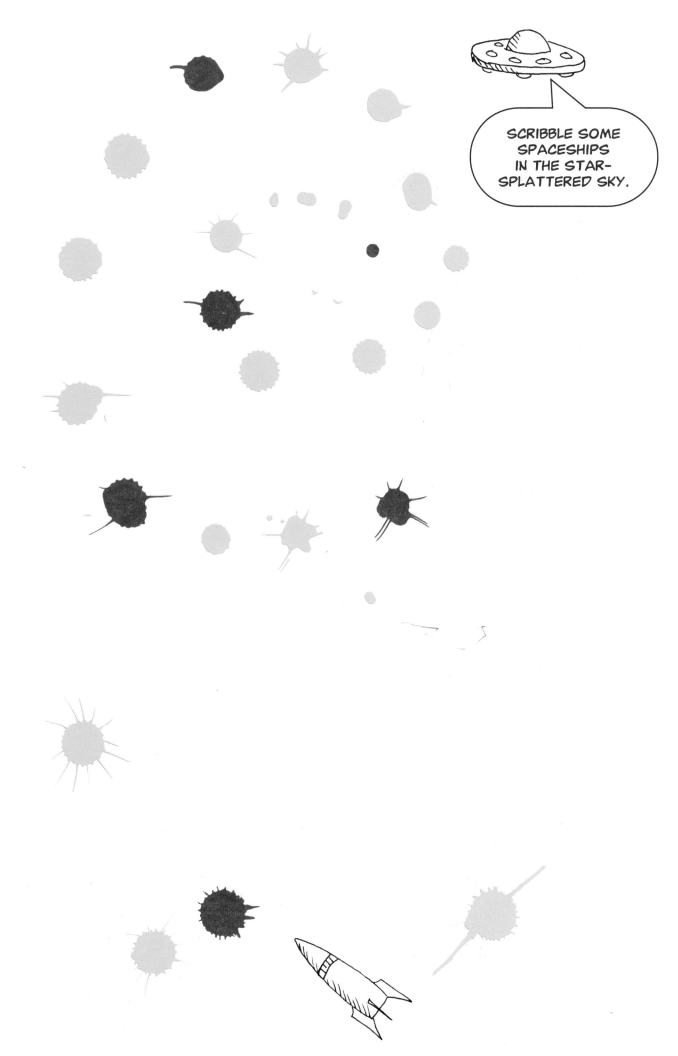

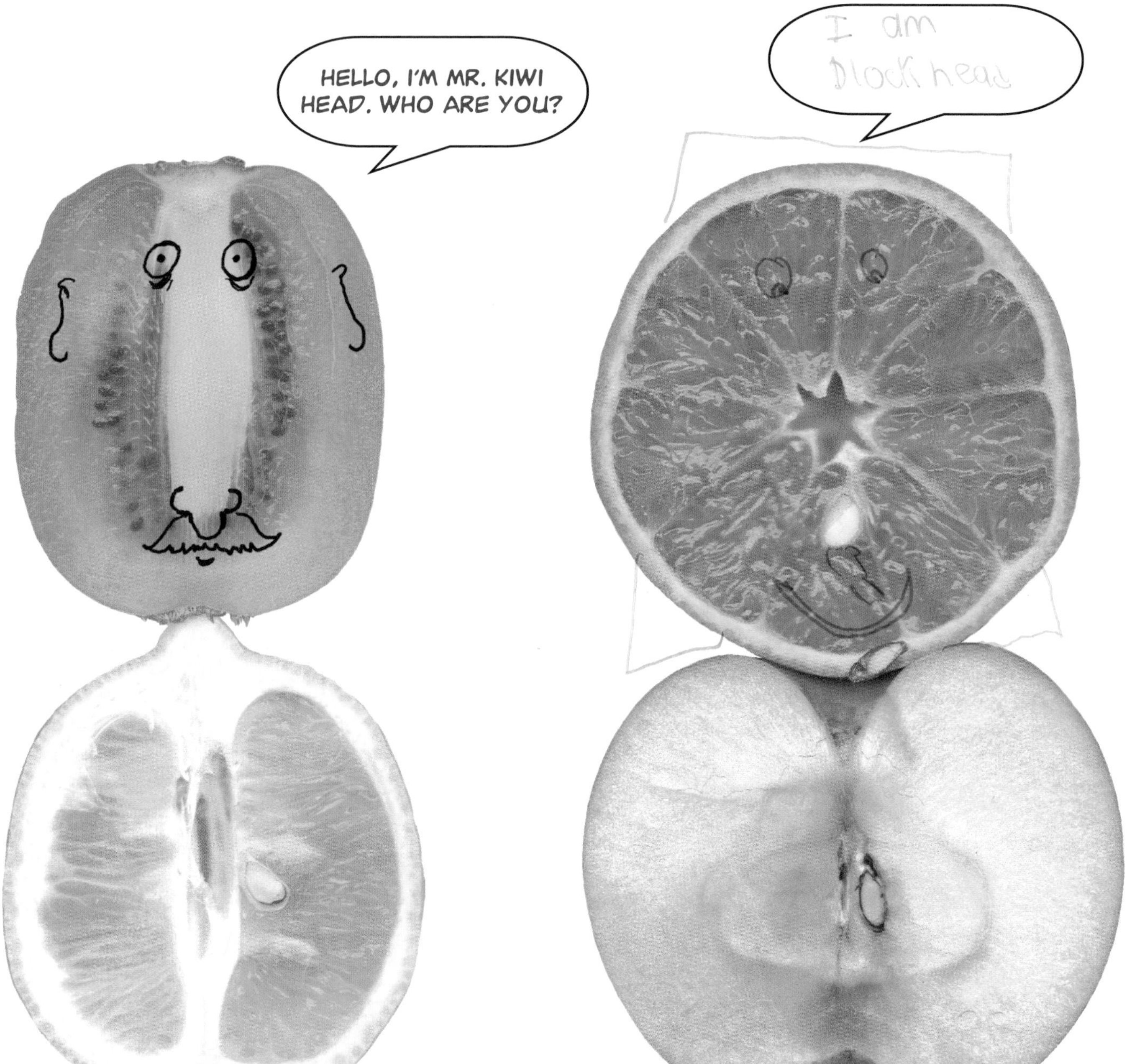
HELLO, I'M MR. KIWI HEAD. WHO ARE YOU?
I am block head

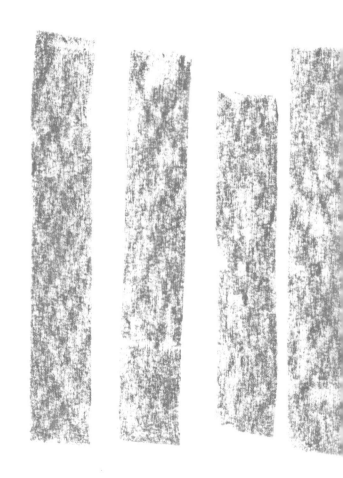

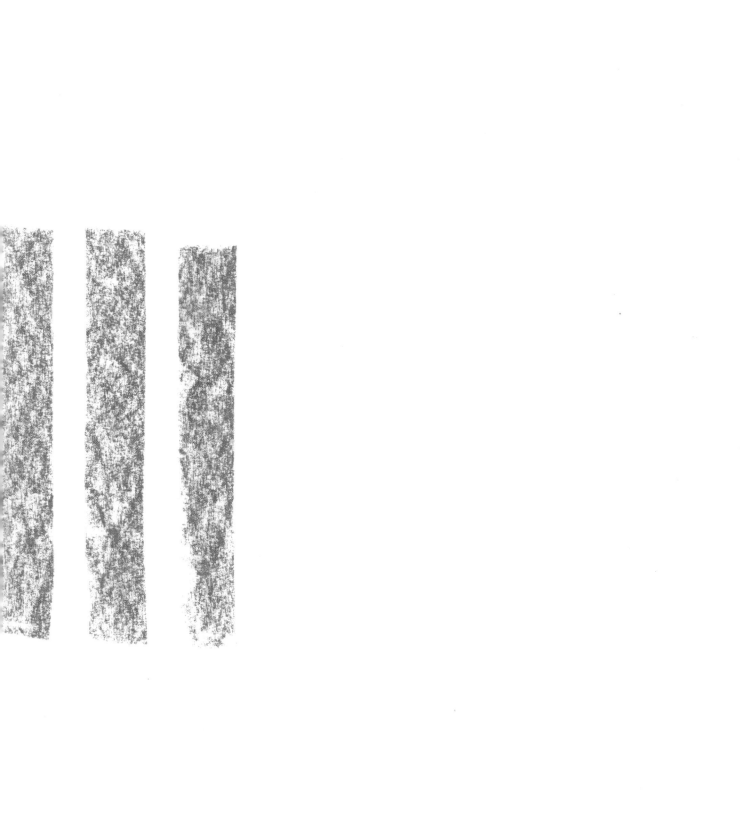

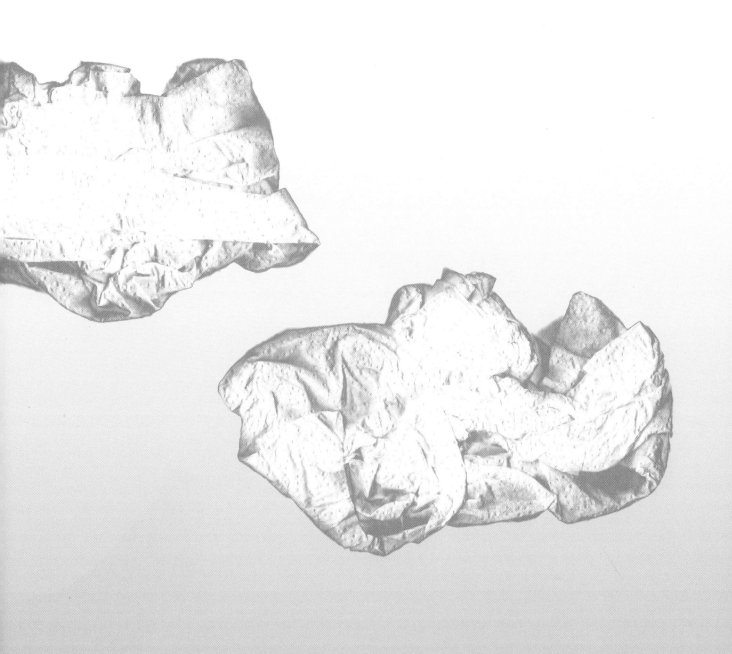

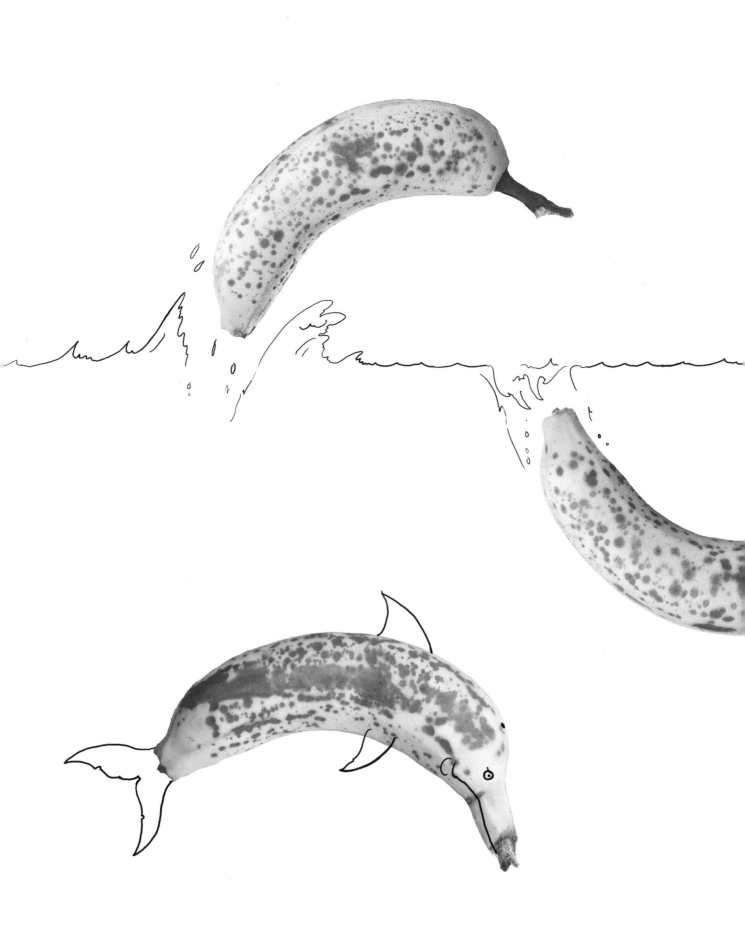

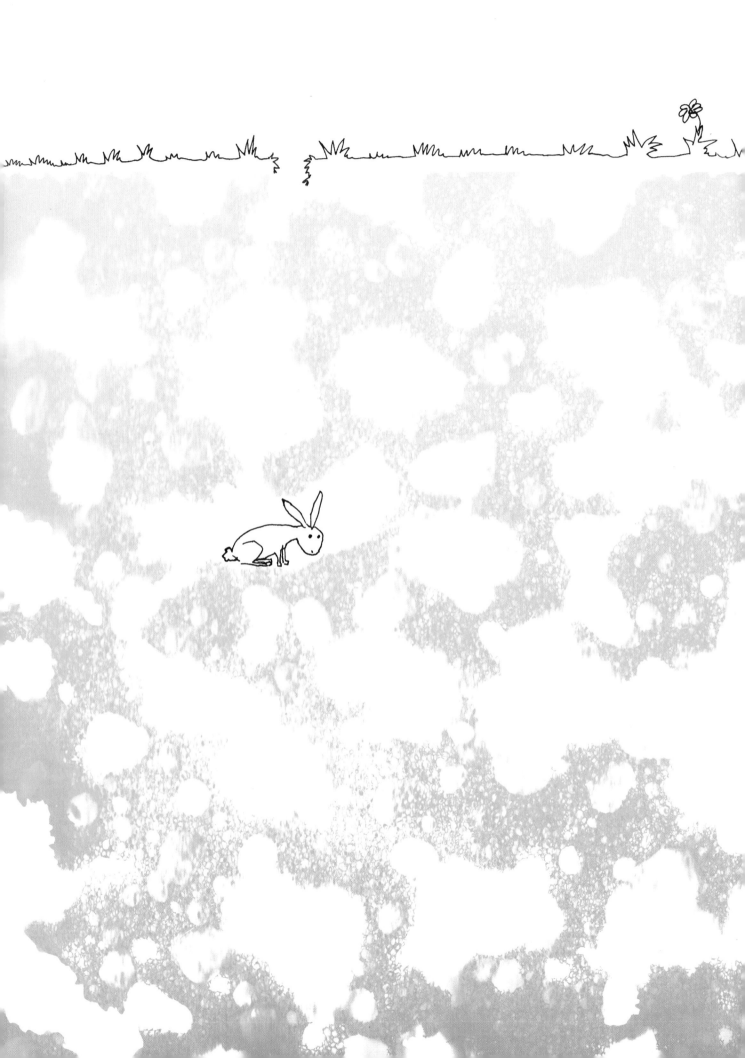

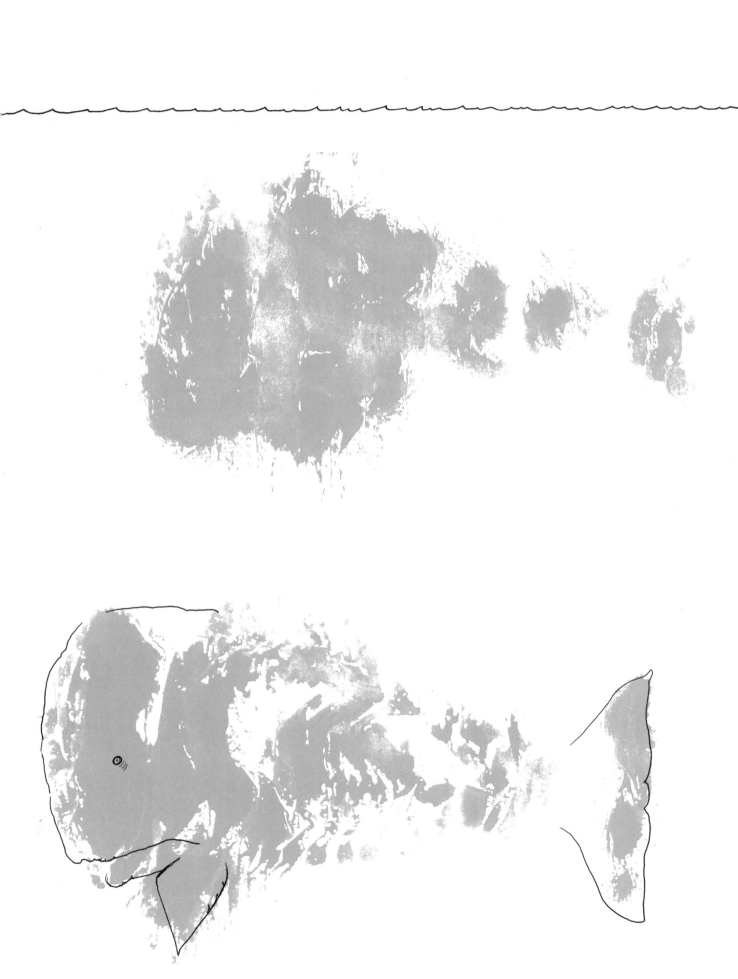

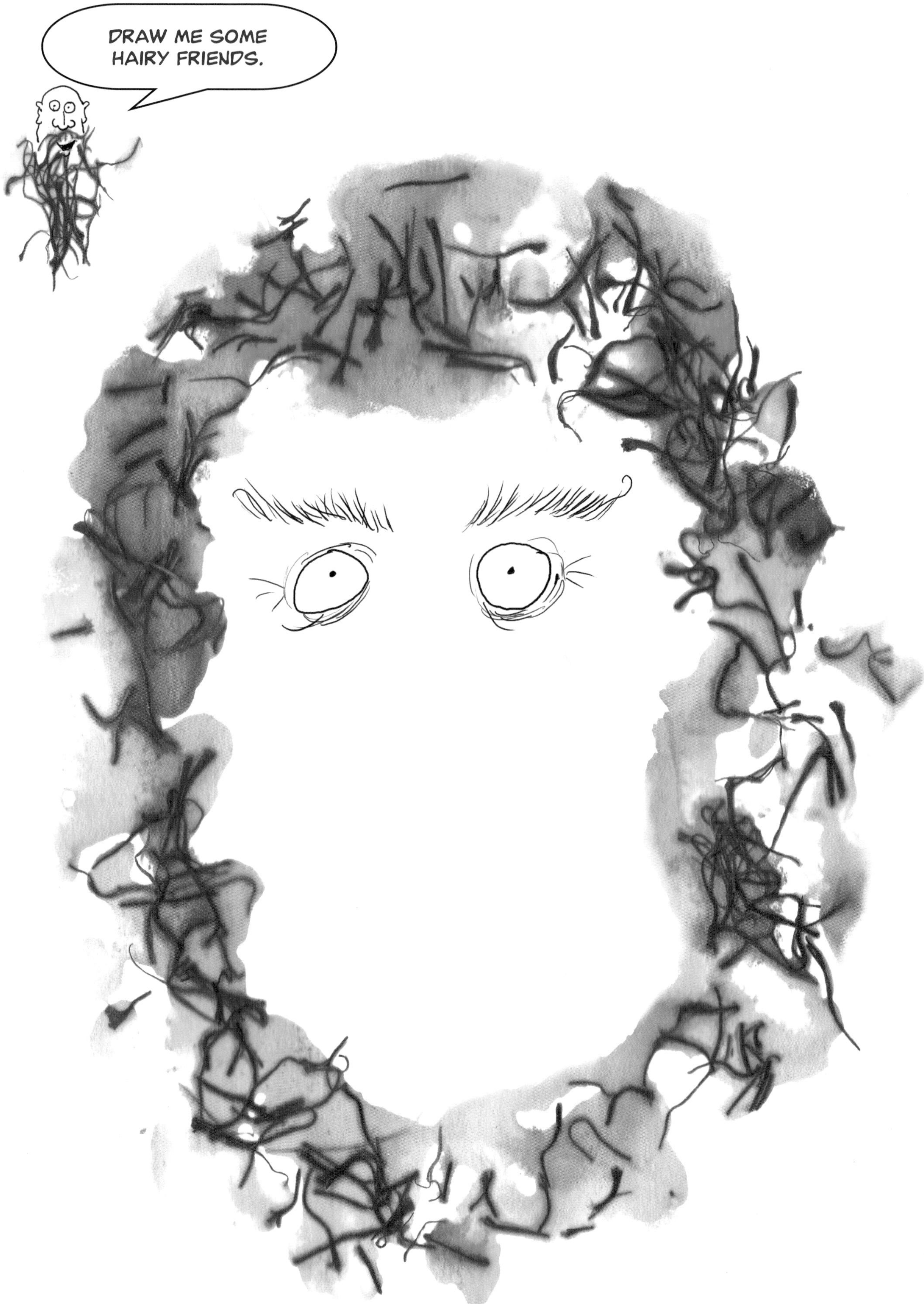
DRAW ME SOME HAIRY FRIENDS.

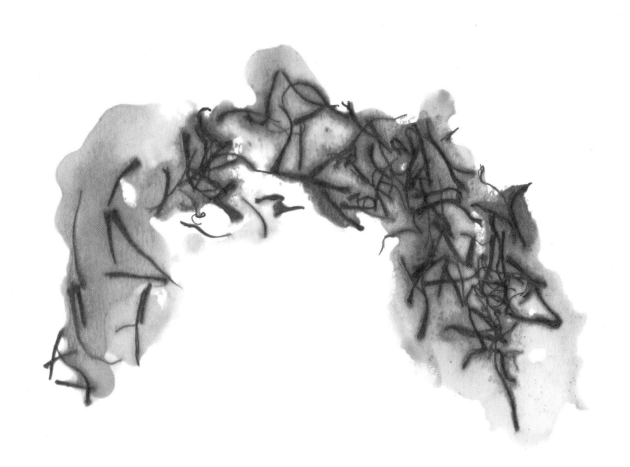

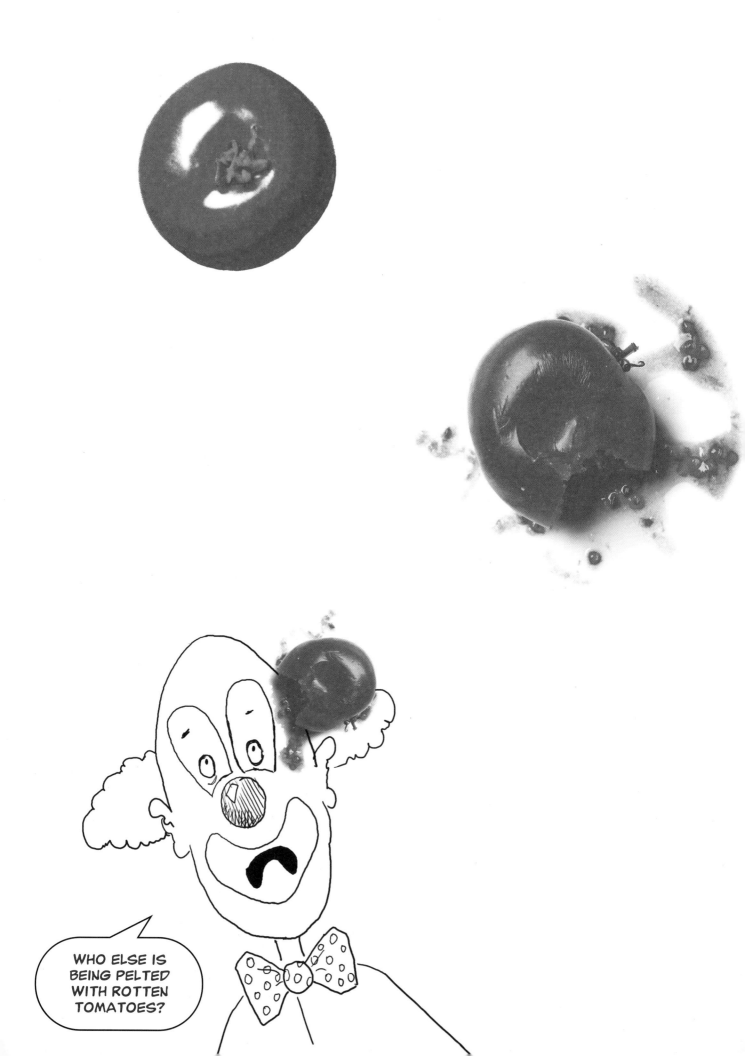

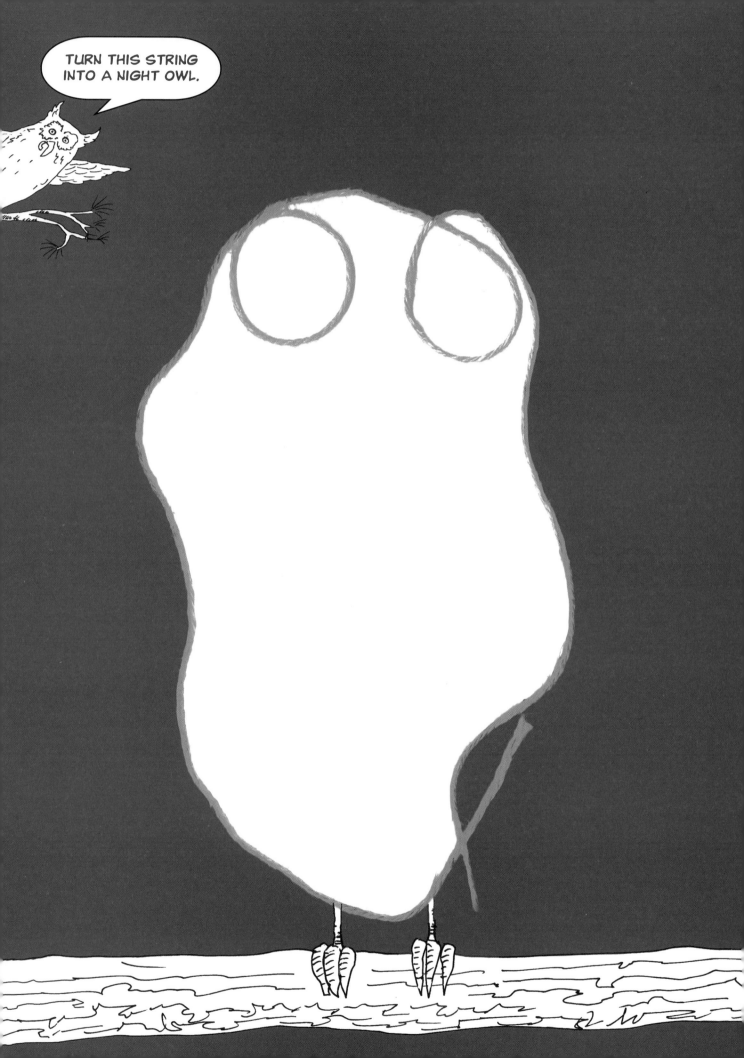

GIVE CRANKY CLAUS SOME COMPANY.

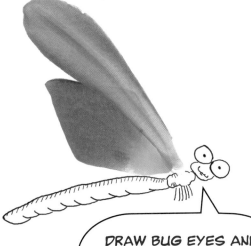

DRAW BUG EYES AND BODIES TO MAKE A FLOCK OF DRAGONFLIES.

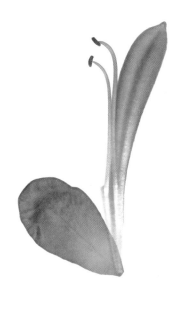

MAKE A TROUPE OF LEAF-HAT DANCERS.